LABOR DAY

by Robin Nelson

Lerner Publications Company · Minneapolis

We **celebrate** Labor Day
every year.

2009 September

SUNDAY	MONDAY	TUESDAY	WEDNESDAY	THURSDAY	FRIDAY	SATURDAY
		1	2	3	4	5
6	7 Labor Day	8	9	10	11	12
13	14	15	16	17	18	19
20	21	22	23	24	25	26
27	28	29	30			

This holiday is on the first Monday in September.

Labor means "work."

Long ago, people worked
long hours for little money.

They worked every day of
the week without much rest.

Even children worked long hours.

One day, some workers did
not go to work.

They **marched** in a parade.

They held signs asking for shorter workdays.

This was the first Labor Day parade.

We celebrate Labor Day in many ways.

We celebrate the end of summer.

We celebrate with family and friends.

We celebrate with parades.

We celebrate everyone who works.

Labor Day gives workers a day of **vacation**.

Labor Day Timeline

September 5, 1882
Workers marched on the first Labor Day in New York City.

September 5, 1883
The second Labor Day was celebrated.

1887
Oregon was the first state to have an official Labor Day.

June 28, 1894
Labor Day became a national holiday.

Labor Day Facts

 About 10,000 workers marched in the first Labor Day parade.

 After the first Labor Day parade, workers met their families in a park for a picnic, concert, and speeches.

 Labor Day is celebrated in September because it is halfway between Independence Day and Thanksgiving.

 Labor Day is also celebrated as the last day of summer.

 President Grover Cleveland signed a law making the first Monday in September Labor Day nationwide.

 Schools, government offices, and most businesses are closed on Labor Day.

 The United States is not the only country that celebrates Labor Day. Labor Day is celebrated in Canada and many other countries.

Glossary

 celebrate – to have a party or special activity to honor a special occasion

 labor – work

 marched – walked in step with others

 vacation – a period of rest

Index

The images in this book are used with the permission of: AP Photo/John Heller, pp. 2, 22 (top); © Independent Picture Service, p. 3; © hana/Datacraft/Getty Images, pp. 4, 22 (second from top); Mid-Manhattan Picture Collection, The New York Public Library, Astor, Lenox and Tilden Foundations, p. 5; The Granger Collection, New York, pp. 6, 11, 22 (third from top); © Hulton Archive/Getty Images, p. 7; Photography Collection, Miriam and Ira D. Wallach Division of Art, Prints and Photographs, The New York Public Library, Astor, Lenox and Tilden Foundations, p. 8; © Bettmann/CORBIS, p. 9; © North Wind Picture Archives, p. 10; © Visual Ideas/Camilo Morales/Getty Images, p. 12; © Jacek Chabraszewski/Shutterstock Images, p. 13; © Ariel Skelley/Getty Images, p. 14; © Black Star/Alamy, p. 15; © Fabrizio Costantini/WpN/UPPA/Photoshot, p. 16; © Jose Luis Pelaez/Photographer's Choice/Getty Images, pp. 17, 22 (bottom).

Front cover: © Thinkstock Images/Getty Images.

Lerner Publications Company
A division of Lerner Publishing Group, Inc.
241 First Avenue North
Minneapolis, MN 55401 U.S.A.

Website address: www.lernerbooks.com

Library of Congress Cataloging-in-Publication Data

Nelson, Robin, 1971–
    Labor Day / by Robin Nelson.
       p.   cm. — (First step nonfiction. American holidays)
    Includes index.
    ISBN 978–0–7613–4933–4 (lib. bdg. : alk. paper)
    1. Labor Day—Juvenile literature. I. Title.
    HD7791.N456 2010
    394.264—dc22   2009010592

Manufactured in the United States of America
1 2 3 4 5 6 – DP – 15 14 13 12 11 10